Samantha Wears a Contact Lens
JUST LIKE YOU!

A day in the life of a unilateral aphakic child

Story by Juliette Vignola
Illustrated by Helen Dwiyanti

This book is dedicated to my silly, sweet Samantha.

This title is also available in French, Italian, and Spanish.

**Other books in the "JUST LIKE YOU!" collection:
Jack Wears Contact Lenses and Glasses...JUST LIKE YOU!
Jack Wears Glasses and a Patch... JUST LIKE YOU!
Everyone's Different... JUST LIKE YOU!**

This book is not intended as a substitute for the medical advice of physicians. The reader should regularly consult a physician in matters relating to his/her health and particularly with respect to any symptoms that may require diagnosis or medical attention.

Copyright © 2013 by Juliette Vignola

ALL RIGHTS RESERVED. This book contains material protected under International and Federal Copyright Laws and Treaties. Any unauthorized reprint or use of this material is prohibited. No part of this book may be reproduced or transmitted in any form or by any means, electronic or mechanical, including photocopying, recording, or by any information storage and retrieval system without express written permission from the author.

This is Samantha!

Samantha likes to read books and play with toys.

**Samantha wears a contact lens in her eye...
JUST LIKE YOU!!**

In the morning, Mommy washes her hands before putting in Samantha's contact lens.
It is very important to keep the contact lens clean!

Step 1: Be very gentle, Mommy!

Step 2: Open wide!

Step 3: Pop it in!

Not so bad!!

Does your Mommy or Daddy put your contact lens in for you?

Sometimes Samantha cannot wear her contact lens. Instead, she wears her glasses. Samantha's glasses are pink! What color are your glasses?

Samantha likes to visit the eye doctor.
The doctor is very nice!
He asks Samantha to keep very still
so that he can look in her eyes.

Before Samantha can go out to play she gets to pick out a super awesome patch! Samantha likes purple patches the best. Which color do you like the best?

Samantha likes for her patch to be the same color as her clothes.

Samantha likes to play outside with her friends. The children wear sunglasses and hats to keep the sun out of their eyes.

At the end of the day it's time to take off the patch. Samantha likes to play peek-a-boo!

"Peek a boo!"

At bedtime, Mommy takes out Samantha's contact lens. But first, she washes her hands really well.

Step 1: Be very gentle, Mommy!

Step 2: Open wide!

Step 3: Pop it out!

Not so bad!!

Sometimes it takes a few tries, and Samantha gets mad. It is not fun to have Mommy poking at her eyes! Sometimes it is hard to cooperate.

**Mommy gives Samantha a big hug
to make her feel better.
Samantha loves hugs, don't you?**

Samantha's contact lens and patch help her to see better.

Lots of children wear contact lenses and glasses. Some children wear a patch too! We are all very lucky we have contact lenses to help us see!

Printed in Great Britain
by Amazon